Designed
IN WHITE

Designed
IN WHITE

LISA LIBELLE

WHITE STAR PUBLISHERS

Contents

Dear Reader,

Perhaps you know already know my name from my blog. Since 2009 I have been sharing
my dreams about interior design and everyday experiences with like-minded people
in my blog *www.lisabelle.com*. I also include photographs there, since in recent years
I have discovered my passion for photography. Since then I have seen the world in a
different light, namely through the viewfinder of my camera. Taking photographs helps
me to capture the beautiful things in life. Among these I have taken so many pictures
in and around my house and in this book I want to show you how you can incorporate
all the beauty around you if you keep your eyes open. I have always had a love of detail.
The love of living in a white atmosphere has been gathering pace in the last few years.

I live with my husband and our three dogs in a terraced family house. The style in
our house has always been modern and purist. I still remember our housewarming

8 Welcome to my white world, in which my dogs feel very much at home!

party very vividly. At the time my mother asked me when the furniture was going to be delivered! The house had very few pieces of furniture, including a few antiques, and the effect was clean and clear—perhaps too a little cold and un-lived in.

Nowadays we could not imagine living like that any more. Instead we enjoy living surrounded by treasures we have found in flea markets and furniture with a beautiful patina! This has completely changed the atmosphere in our house. Now you really feel you are immersed in happiness. The dominant color is white, combined with wonderful nuances of ivory and cream, often enhanced by touches of soft shades of pastel. The light is reflected throughout the house thanks to the white that is everywhere. Even on grey winter days, white lights up the house and helps us survive the gloom of that season. The mixture of shabby chic, some vintage touches, French country style and the Scandinavian look is present throughout the house. All this conjures up the charm of days gone by and a touch of dreamy romanticism! I love everything that is nostalgic and have done since I was a little girl. Ballet and the piano have always been my passion and they still are. I wanted to be a ballerina, later a visual merchandiser, a writer, an actress or a wedding organizer but things can always change. That is my motto. In this book I have tried to share with you all my dreams of living in a perfect home through pictures, proverbs, thoughts and tips. I hope that my dreams come across in this book.
With my best wishes,

LISA LIBELLE

$\mathcal{L}$ive your dreams and love your home. It reflects your personality. Make sure that it is a faithful reflection and that it will strengthen your affection.

WHITE INSPIRATIONS

My house ...

... is there where I walk through the rooms and I feel on a white cloud. The color white is like a balm for the soul. It conveys tranquil energy and at the same time it radiates calm. The decision to transform our house into a white dream house is one that I have never regretted and would make again. White furniture and white decoration look perfect throughout the house and the color white is like a blank canvas for the artist. White is pure, delicate, calming and refreshing. And there are many shades of white. Look closely at your surroundings and you will certainly notice how true this is. From pure white to nuances of

12 The elegant dresser with scroll details is a dream for every romantic heart. As well as showing off the old telephone, it can also be decorated as you wish. The little old suitcase is a place where our four-legged friends can relax. In keeping with the style of the mattress, it has a white lace cover. The mirror with its black frame is a dark, contrasting accent in the decor.

13 An antique pocket watch is timeless and very decorative. Sometimes it is the little things that make a uniquely charming decoration. Here the lace ribbon and pearls make this nostalgic accessory look ev eingefasst en more romantic.

14 Here a simple notebook has been decorated with a piece of a musical score and some lace, giving it a romantic, shabby-chic style.

ivory, cream or buttermilk. Depending on how the paint is applied, it creates a feeling of wellbeing and encourages positive thinking.

What is so inspiring about white surroundings in your house is that white can be combined with any color, so a few dashes of color will immediately alter the mood and atmosphere in a room. Lovingly chosen details and decorative objects can also play an important part. So depending on your mood or on the season, you can create a completely different atmosphere in the house from one day to another by adding a few cushions, some flowers or some decorations you have made yourself. I absolutely love the 1,001 little treasures I have collected and I am convinced that they contribute to the positive mood of my home, because everything around us has a soul, even a bedside table or a washbowl.

For me, the most beautiful thing about white surroundings is that all the white elements reflect the light. A house suffused with light is like poetry. In northern latitudes where the dark winter months linger much too long, white is a very popular color for that very reason. On gloomy days this reflected light emanates positive energy, providing the strength to overcome the sadness of winter. Just try it, with one or two pieces of white-colored furniture in a room you will immediately not only see the reflection of the light but feel it! Have I made you curious? In that case, just follow "white color" therapy in your own home: the results will amaze you.

Old postcards, some delicious pastry and fragrant flowers from the garden will create a delightful, romantic atmosphere. Have a good look at all your "junk" and you will find numerous little gems that will make delightful decorative objects.

THE LIVING ROOM –
the heart of the house

The whole family gets together in the living-room. By using bedspreads and removable sofa covers, white in the house can co-exist with children and animals.

SEL AUX HERBES
20 KG. NET

1000

19 left The old typewriter adds a touch of history
to the living room. A quill pen and ink are ready too,
because it is much more personal to write
your cards and letters by hand.

19 right Toys such as a teddy bear or rocking horse
introduce a playful note into the house.
Combined with flowers,
they become romantic.

18 The concept of matching shades works like a symphony of colors. Old flour sacks or new reproductions such as these by "Jeanne d'Arc Living" protect the light-colored upholstery of the romantic armchair and add a touch of French country style. The cushions with the franked stamps and handwritten addresses complete the picture.

THE LIVING ROOM must be a place to relax. The living room is where you read your favorite book, enjoy a cup of tea or have a short nap depending on the time of day and your mood.

A comfortable living room means that it must have the right conditions for every mood, for instance a little table with two chairs near the window where you can enjoy a cup of coffee in the afternoon, or a comfortable armchair near the fire that will invite you to dream in winter. Having several sofas and armchairs will allow the family to use the room individually while making it a haven of well-being for the whole family.

White is anything but boring! Whether eggshell, pure white or creamy: the color white reflects the light and is a balm for the soul. Let yourself be inspired by the various shades of white and design the house of your dream completely in white! White tablecloths, covers, cushions and accessories with lace, beads and crochet embroidery complete the romantic touch.

22 top Picturesque flower arrangements! Flowers create a romantic atmosphere throughout the house. Large bunches of flowers look great in zinc buckets that are in perfect harmony with the shabby-chic style. The ornate birdcage in the background enhances the romantic atmosphere.

22 bottom left Our pug Mai-Lin also loves her white surroundings and, being very curious, she loves exploring her domain.

22 bottom right Whether filled with seasonal flowers, Christmas baubles or strips of manuscript paper, soup tureens in various sizes are an excellent basis for romantic decorations. You can add a touch of elegance by tying satin or lace ribbons onto the handles. Such decorations can be made in no time at all and the effect is fantastic!

The Madonna is one of my favorite objects in the house. Whether an antique wooden sculpture or a modern variation like this one, made of china—the expression on the Madonna's face is both gentle and pensive, giving the room a special atmosphere.

White and cream tones as well as many ancient and nostalgic elements are what make this country kitchen charming.

THE KITCHEN –
charming, small and pretty

26 top left Old cooky cutters look very decorative and add a special touch to the kitchen at any time, not just at Christmas!

26 top right The old cooker hood has been painted a matching creamy-white color and decorated with various objects.

26 bottom left Fresh flowers also look very good in a kitchen. A simple yogurt jar or jam jar will make a very decorative vase.

26 bottom right Always close at hand! Practical decorative items should be usable every day as well as being beautiful.

WITH A LOT OF IMAGINATION and well-thought out ideas, even the smallest room can become the heart of the house. Light-colored cupboards and country-style objects will make a small kitchen look bigger as well as friendly. Mirrors also work wonders in a dark room because they reflect the light. At first our kitchen was modern and very minimalist. But what we really wanted was a cozy farmhouse kitchen. So the first thing we did was to replace the high gloss cupboard doors with cream-colored paneled ones with ceramic handles. Old white-painted wooden stools added to the farmhouse look as did the old kitchen table. An old shelf on the wall was perfect for kitchen utensils.

Then instead of keeping storage jars, dishes and kitchen tools in cupboards and drawers, in a shabby-look style kitchen they are exposed to view because they create a nostalgic and romantic atmosphere. Dark-colored touches such

Who could resist these adorable lacy tops? In no time at all these simple jars have been transformed into the most charming decorative objects with an atmosphere all their own.

as wire and zinc containers or the ancient madeleine mold in discolored metal introduce a contrasting note, as does the dark kitchen floor. You do not need much to create a pleasant country-style kitchen: you kind find kitchen utensils such as an enamel sieve or glass containers, reminiscent of days gone by, in furniture stores. Fittings, sinks and even very modern kitchen equipment such as induction hobs and toasters are also available in retro-style, thus adding a nostalgic charm to the kitchen. Then you can add the final touch by adding a few smaller items of furniture or selected decorative items from the flea market or a secondhand shop.

The kitchen towels and crockery in the white-painted cupboard are within easy reach.

The basic color in the kitchen is white. A few dark touches such as the traditional madeleine mould, reminiscent of France, sets off the white background.

Even a small kitchen can become a family kitchen with the right decorative accessories. The old kitchen utensils hanging on the wall are within easy reach and their slightly nostalgic worn appearance conjures up images of country kitchens of the past. The small table with the bench and cushion against the wall invite the family to share in a cozy meal. Fresh wild flowers transform the room into a charming farmhouse kitchen.

THE DINING ROOM
– a touch of aristocracy

30-31 The inviting dining room has enough room for a pleasant social gatherings. Guests can dine in style at the large dining table but there is also space to make still life arrangements based on the theme of food.

32-33 With elegant flatware and beautiful crockery, every table can become a banqueting table. The glass butter dish has a nostalgic charm and goes perfectly with the period flatware.

Things are never what they are. You are always what you make of them.

JEAN ANOUILH

34 top left Flatware can be anywhere, not just on the table ! A white-painted wreath on the door, to which the spoon and fork are attached with a piece of lace, points the way to the dining room. Flea markets are an ideal source of silver flatware.

34 top right Antique gems alongside mouthwatering delicacies and a touch of imagination: the sideboard is an ideal place to display some of your older treasures.

34 bottom left The dining room has the air of a grand hotel where coffee and tea are served in small silver pots. So with a few accessories every home, whether large or small, simple or aristocratic, can become one's own grand hotel.

34 bottom right Spring enters the house with the first flowers. Using plants, flowers and scattered decorations, you can create a beautiful Easter decoration for the table.

35 Old treasures from the flea market give a unique fasciantion to the surroundings!

IN OUR DINING ROOM the table is decorated every day because you do not need a special occasion to create an atmospheric table decoration. Depending on the season you can conjure up the most magnificent decoration in no time at all, making it a pleasure for family and guests to be gathering the table to enjoy some delicacies. Decorate the table with elegant napkins, candlesticks and fresh, fragrant pastel-colored flowers to welcome family and guests. The room emanates an elegance and a mood that invite guests to linger. The friendly and to some extent slightly ostentatious interior in cozy shades of white is reminiscent of a grand hotel and so creates a timeless, elegant atmosphere. The many touches of shabby-chic elements, such as the antique mirror with a gilt frame, hanging above the table, add a subtly aristocratic note. This large mirror reflects the daylight and in the evening it reflects the light of the chandelier with its elegant silhouette, thus creating a unique play of light.

THE BEDROOM –
a haven of peace

The bedroom is the most private room in the house. Use your imagination and decorate this room to your own very personal taste— and you can be sure of having sweet dreams.

Old mannequins are not always easy to find. But with a little imagination, even a modern one can soon be turned into an eye-catching decorative object. With a white lacy top, wings and feminine accessories such as pearl necklaces, this mannequin clearly symbolizes a guardian angel.

39 top left Personal elements such as the
wedding dress, decorated with angels' wings,
hanging from the cupboard, evoke memories
of the most beautiful moments in life.

39 top right A dream of days gone by, this old
white-painted mirror with its beautiful
patina is used as a make-up mirror and
as a place to hang jewelry..

OUR BEDROOM had to have a romantic atmosphere, being a room that is dedicated
to love and angels. The pale-colored, romantic furnishings invite us to dream and to linger.
The white-painted furniture and the mirror make the room look bigger. Seasonal fresh flowers
in white and pastel shades add a cheerful note to the room and make it look lively.
The romantic atmosphere of the bedroom is enhanced by a few words of love that have
been painted on the walls and cupboards. The numerous angel figures are not only beautiful
to look at but they should also protect us in our sleep during the night. Further memorabilia
and objects with their own history decorate the shelves and chest of drawers as a still life
and turn the bedroom into a haven of personal wellbeing.

40 An old mirror adds a decorative note to the little chest of drawers. As well as the light, it reflects the delicate flowers adorning the chest.

---

41 top White furniture and accessories make the room look bigger. The flowers, soft fabrics and a decorative counterpane add to the romantic atmosphere.

---

41 bottom This display cabinet was once painted cream and in the family room. After a coat of white paint, it is now used to store freshly ironed bedspreads and sheets. The glass doors of the cabinet have been decorated with sheer curtains to conceal the contents.

Treat yourself to some
time out! Allow yourself to
dream and recharge your
batteries in a voluptuous
fragrant, romantically
decorated bath.

THE BATHROOM
– a place for body and soul

44 top left A white mug is perfect for keeping makeup tools.

44 top right Bathroom fittings are also available in retro versions. They convey a touch of nostalgia to the bathroom.

44 bottom left Romantic decorations and fresh flowers are always welcome in the bathroom.

44 bottom right A soothing, exfoliating lavender sea salt body scrub is very relaxing.

45 The old zinc bucket is ideal for storing reserve rolls of toilet paper and it also adds a touch of nostalgia.

ACCESSORIES ADD STYLE and give the bathroom a personal touch. I like to have pleasant objects and romantic ones in the bathroom. When I lie in the bath and dream, I love looking at the decorations, accessories and ornaments around me and they fill me with delight. I believe mussels and pearls belong in a bathroom. These gifts of nature remind me of the wonderful moments I have spent by the sea. There are many myths about pearls and in several cultures they represent purity, wisdom and femininity. Refreshing perfumes and soaps remind me of a flowering meadow, while roses, decorative glasses and candles add a romantic touch. A crystal chandelier gives the bathroom a regal air while retro-style fittings add a touch of class. So a modern bathroom can easily be transformed into an elegant room.

From A
LOVE OF DETAIL

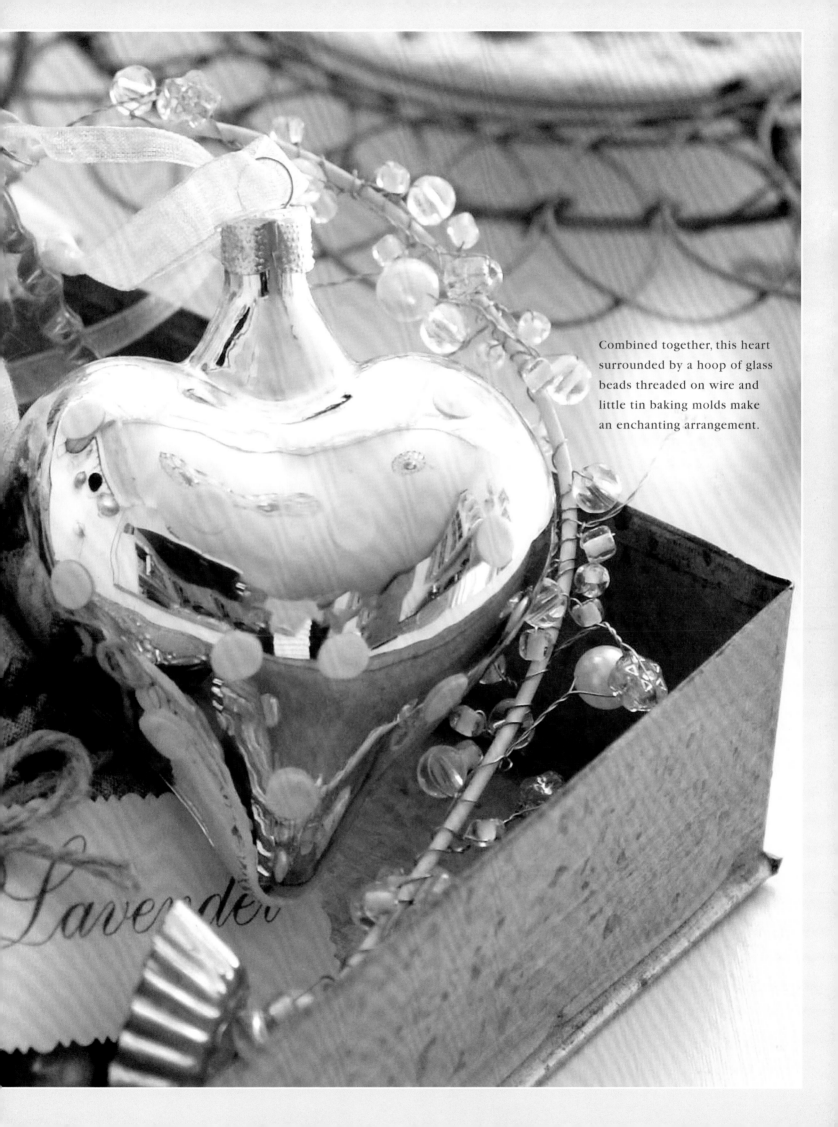

Combined together, this heart surrounded by a hoop of glass beads threaded on wire and little tin baking molds make an enchanting arrangement.

Romanticism and Nostalgia

What would life be without passion? For me, it would be like a book without a proper ending, a life without charisma or an existence without excitement. Life is much too short to spend it exclusively with duties and obligations and without passionate enthusiasm. Live every day with a dash of passion and supplement it with romanticism and nostalgia. Discover what makes you happy and what makes your heart beat faster.

Think about what touches your soul. Passion enlivens our life and invites us to see the world through different eyes. When you remember the happiest moments in your life, let these memories inspire you in the organization and decoration of your home. The love of details will transform your house into a place full of passion and warmth, keeping alive the happiest moments of your life. If you design and decorate with your heart, everything will be right!

48 It would be a shame to hide personal treasures such as letters and little cards away in drawers.

49 In summer nature provides us with luxuriant flowers. A heavenly individual rose in an old Champagne glass adds a romantic touch to the surroundings.

Old jewelry and framed photographs with a patina and a history create a wonderful effect. With a bit of luck you will find wonderful little trinkets like these in flea markets and antique shops.

LACE AND FLOWERS

What is more romantic than the finest lace combined with delicate flowers? Lace is ideal if want to add a touch of nostalgia to your ornaments and furniture. If you do not know how to crochet yourself, find some old lace and crochet trimmings in flea markets. Existing lace trimming on old bed linen and handkerchiefs can easily be reused. Old lace look great when combined with old jewelry. Or arrange medallions, old postcards and small trinkets together with old lace. In an instant you can create a vintage decorative composition that is unique and extremely romantic. Complete your still life with fresh flowers— a delightful effect!

52 top Spoil yourself with linen bed sheets. Old sheets with lace trimmings are extremely decorative and give the house a nostalgic charm, whether used as decorative drapes, tablecloths or sofa covers.

52 bottom left A passionate decoration! Lingerie trimmed with lace and pearls and combined with flower petals and trinkets makes a truly passionate decoration! When brought together, these elements create a genuinely romantic, feminine atmosphere.

52 bottom right A white-painted pitcher, a hand-embroidered linen towel and a flower from the garden! This makes a refreshing, fragrant decoration that invites you to dream wherever it is.

53 These hand-crocheted baskets from my studio were first dipped in a water and sugar solution, then left to harden. Several such decorations placed in the living room create an atmospheric decoration with a calming light.

You can conjure up the most beautiful decorations for the house and garden with gypsophila. Whether as little wreaths to decorate the backs of chairs or to use as table decorations—let yourself to be inspired by these filigree plants!

DO YOU LOVE GYPSOPHILA AS MUCH AS I DO? The name of the plant alone Gypsophila elegans makes you dream. The "elegans" in the name is perfect because gypsophila is such a graceful plant. Its common name "baby's breath" is also charmingly evocative. In spite of its daintiness with its small, white flowers, it is robust and easy to look after, which is why it is one of the most cultivated cut flowers. And brides often decide to include gypsophila in their wedding bouquet. Gypsophila always looks elegant with its small white flowers reminiscent of delicate pearls or tiny snowflakes. The pink variety is also very picturesque.

55 Gypsophila is very versatile and it looks deliciously languorous. Hand-made wreaths of gypsophila last for a very long time and they are always beautiful to look at. Small wreaths look very decorative placed on furniture or other items such as a small, shabby-looking white-painted chicken coop or elegant butter dishes with silver lids. The little gypsophila flowers looking like tiny snowflakes are very dainty and romantic.

56-57 As delicate as a bridal bouquet, these cream-colored freshly cut roses are tied together with lace trimmings from an old sheet secured with pearl-headed pins. The delicate lace bedspread, like those our great-grandmothers used, and a few elegant accessories such as the filigree wire basket, the lace ribbon and a ball of string create a romantic, feminine atmosphere.

Give every day the chance to become the most beautiful of your life.

MARK TWAIN

59 left Spring flowers, a cream-colored purse decorated with flounces and a stylish modern cup together create a harmonious, atmospheric tone-on-tone decorative arrangement.

59 right Skirts and clothes with flounces and ruffles in delicate colors, hanging from a cupboard or door, look very decorative.

58 This old chair, covered with a luxurious cushion decorated with flounces, creates a pure, romantic impression. Fragrant lilac flowers from the garden enhance this unique effect.

FLOUNCES ARE NOSTALGIC and very decorative. I often use linen and clothes with flounces as decoration. Flounces are like a romance for the heart, like a poetic ode to the home. These very light fabrics with ruffles combine languorous elegance and girly playfulness. Combined with flowers and shabby-look accessories, they create a nostalgic still life. Magnificent cushions with flounces give a look of days gone by to the sofa and to the bedroom. You can decorate everything with flounces—they always look magically romantic and playful.

ENCHANTED BY THE BLAZE OF LIGHT

Light is a wonderful gift of nature. It is amazingly beautiful as reflected in the way the light changes according to the seasons. Light is like a balm for the body and soul. For instance, have you noticed how your mood can suddenly change because of the light? When the sun shines we feel full of joie de vivre. The rays of the sun transform our thoughts into projects, hopes and positive thinking. Nature shows us how to do it. Flowers need the sun in order to flower. People need light in order to live. Light can be a wonderful source of inspiration. Bright light heightens the mood. On the other hand, gloomy light leads to melancholy. Surroundings and atmosphere also change when the light changes… each light creates its own atmosphere. Let yourself be inspired by nature!

60 Old glasses in various sizes, arranged on a silver tray, can make a very elegant centerpiece for the table. Acting as cut-crystal lanterns, they reflect and disperse the light of the candles, creating a dream-like atmosphere in the dining room.

61 This sea-related shabby-look decoration creates a magic atmosphere in the evening. The jam jars and yogurt jars are perfect for making subtle atmospheric lanterns. They will enable you to spend pleasant evenings outside, dreaming of your last holiday by the sea. The soft candlelight calms the senses.

62 top left A delicate pocket watch with its chain turns a simple bell glass into an elegant object.

62 top right A new clock with a design from the past, showing obvious (albeit faked) marks of age. The Roman numerals are appropriate for the shabby-chic look of this charming farmhouse clock.

62 bottom left This old pocket watch with an engraved monogram is full of nostalgia,. It will have been a real pleasure to check the time on it.

62 bottom right Old and new in a harmonious combination: the new alarm clock with its retro look on your night table side by side with an old Omega pocket watch.

63 And time stands still! Dials in various sizes waiting to be used in the next decorative scheme. Even as they are, they are already a decorative eye-catcher.

TAKE YOUR TIME AND GIVE TIME A MEANING How much time does life give us? Do we fill our time meaningfully and do we organize our time purposefully? Have you ever asked yourself what you are doing with this most precious gift of life? "People have no time because they do not take the time to have time." Whoever gives us time gives us the most precious gift on earth. Spending time together, enjoying time together is a wonderful experience. But we can also spend time on our own and give a different meaning to this kind of time. The wonderful thing is that everyone gives time a different meaning. While some people spend a lot of their time reading, others enjoy sporting activities, cooking, baking, painting or dancing. In fact, it does not matter how we spend our time, the most important thing is that we should enjoy what we are doing. So give yourself and your beloved that most precious thing: time.

Oggi apro le mie ali
E sento che domani
l'uomo volerà
stretto nell' abbraccio
di una donna che l'ama...

WRITINGS
& ANNOTATIONS

What is more exciting than recording memories and thoughts
in pretty notebooks? It would be sad if they got lost as so
often happens with beautiful dreams … Take the time and
remember your last holiday. Often what we remember are
the little things that remain engraved forever in our heart
and soul. But beautiful moments need not just be recorded
in notebooks. Why not in the form of a loving message
on a mirror? Or on the floor in the living room, or on the
kitchen wall, or on the front door? Your guests will be
pleasantly surprised and the joie de vivre emanating from
your surroundings will spread to those around you.

Little ways of keeping personal notes: take time to record your thoughts in pretty notebooks. Lovely shabby-look bookmarks will help you locate particular notes.

An old pitcher bought in a flea
market, beautiful spring flowers and
a vintage quill pen highlight the
romantic atmosphere of the house.

67 top Pure nostalgia! This old suitcase is the perfect place for Moro the mongrel to relax. He loves to snuggle in the flounces of the cover. He is sure to have sweet dreams there!

---

67 bottom The text written by hand on the floor tiles of the living room are a source of inspiration. The elegant pumps bring life to the place and are unusually decorative at the same time.

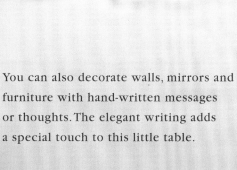

You can also decorate walls, mirrors and furniture with hand-written messages or thoughts. The elegant writing adds a special touch to this little table.

A FASCINATION WITH FLOWERS Imagine life without flowers. Or a house or a garden without the magic of flowers. I love my romantic home with its dainty details and fresh flowers. Naturally I prefer white flowers but I also like flowers in delicate pastel shades such as pale pink and salmon. It is heavenly to be greeted with the fragrance of flowers when you enter a house. My favorite flowers are roses with their delicious fragrance and sumptuous blooms. But I have also a soft spot for ranunculus with their delicate colors, French tulips, hyacinths with their spring fragrance, gypsophila or wild flowers… in other words, I love flowers. Often in a flower shop I cannot decide which flowers to buy. In fact I would like to take every one of them home and turn them into beautiful floral decoration.

To this very day I remember how I felt when I discovered my favorite flower shop completely by chance. While strolling

Flowers
are nature's thoughts of love.

BETTINA VON ARNIM

68 The old piano is the main actor in this floral play. The grand piano is a uniquely decorative display surface for flowers, pictures and tea lights.

69 Small trinkets are even more effective under glass. Delicate bell jars evoke life in a romantic chateau.

71 Romantic dresses always make a room seem nostalgic. This delicate, feminine dress with satin details goes perfectly with the things in the cupboard. Dried flower wreaths in soft colors and a delicate fresh flower arrangement complete the decoration. Poetry for the senses!

70 bottom I give you my heart! Selected objects such as this heart-shaped metal box with ornate decorations will make every rose-lover's heart beat faster.

through the town my attention was caught by a little vaulted room. I felt as if I had been struck by lightning. As I walked by I saw large chandeliers, a table with the patina of age and lovely farmhouse chairs in pastel grey. On the large vintage table were a wealth of flowers and delightful shabby-look objects. I could not believe my eyes, I was so amazed. In a corner stood an old black grand piano, adorned with candlesticks, flowers, wreaths and lanterns. The magic and magnificence of this space was reflected in a huge mirror. On the other side stood an old shabby-style buffet cabinet with its doors open, filled with white porcelain objects. On the walls were pictures of delicate flowers. The atmosphere in this flower shop was so romantic and feminine that it made this shabby-look lover's heart beat faster. The flower shop of your dreams. I knew immediately that this would be my favorite flower shop. Immerse yourself in the world of flowers and discover your favorite flower shop where you will feel like *Alice in Wonderland!*

THE GARDEN OF DREAMS

72-73 A place to dream. The air is filled with the fragrance of spring and all the trees and shrubs are covered with buds. The romantic white tulle curtain on the tree is like a doorway to happiness.

74 The queen of flowers transforms this prety birdbath into a place where little birds can come and rest.

Do you ...

like to dream? Dreams are limitless, everything is allowed in dreams. And not only at night—day dreams are wonderful too. Arrange a meeting with yourself and send your thoughts on a wonderful dream journey. You do not have to feel as if you were in heaven… just look for a quiet corner that will inspire you. This little corner could be in your own garden under a romantic magnolia tree, a lovers' bench in the nearby park or a cozy armchair in the conservatory. When was the last time you watched the clouds go by in the sky or recognize animal shapes in the clouds as you did when you were child? How long since you picked a bunch of flowers and decorated your favorite room to turn it into a romantic haven? Every day we are surrounded by so many beautiful things that are simply there waiting to be discovered. People who go through life with their eyes open will find inspiration everywhere. Live your dream and create your personal dream corner, embellished with romantic decorations.

75 The magnolia is the queen of the realm of flowering shrubs. Its scent appeals to every romantic heart.

$\mathscr{T}he$ best thing that can happen to anyone: when reality is transformed into a dream.

BARON PHILIPPE DE ROTHSCHILD

76 top Do sit down! Fragrant roses, a white cushion and a little parasol create a romantic arrangement on the elegant garden bench.

76 bottom Who could resist such love? Cats are perfect companions for romantic daydreamers, emanating calm while conveying moments of intense emotion.

77 Sensual romanticism! There is a subtle association between the sweet meringue and the English rose "Mary Rose" resting on the dainty rose pastry. Just try it too!

78 top Moments full of poetry: the romantic peonies in shades of delicate pink and the white stone bust of a little girl dreaming form a wonderfully beautiful decorative arrangement.

78 bottom Nothing could be more spring like! This romantic still life with a bunch of ranunculi in pale pastel colors creates a seductive, dreamy atmosphere. Don't worry, the white doves won't fly away!

79 A little paradise by the magnolia. The romantic arrangement of fragrant flowers and wire mannequins, decorated with pearl necklaces and lace ribbon, invites us to dream.

80-81 The green outdoors. In summer you can at last go out again to soak up the sun and fresh air! The elegant white of the china jug reflects each ray of sun and puts one in a good mood.

A romantic
PICNIC

A picnic ...

... in idyllic surroundings, on the edge of a wood, in a meadow or in your own garden is simply heavenly. Give free rein to your imagination and create a delicious menu that seduce the senses! The smell of freshly cut grass, the warmth of the sun on your skin, the buzzing of insects in the air: picnicking is a feast for the senses and an unforgettable experience. Picnicking always reminds me of those wonderful days of my childhood because in summer my family often enjoyed picnics with friends. Today when I close my eyes, I can still hear the bubbling of the stream and the rustling of the leaves in the woods, and I can still smell the delicious fragrance of the food. And I still enjoy these happy moments today. Whether under a tree, in the middle of a flower meadow or in my own garden, there is always a favorite spot for a successful picnic. It is even better if you can bicycle to your picnic. The refreshing air as you cycle along puts you in a good mood and the anticipation of all that delicious food gets even greater as you approach your chosen picnic area.

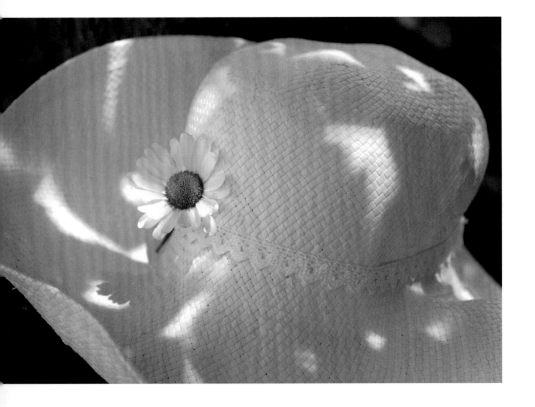

82 The white sun hat is decorated with a lace ribbon embellished with a freshly picked ox-eye daisy. Let the sun shine!

83 You could not imagine a picnic without a basket full of delicious food. The basket should also contain glasses, flatware, crockery, crisp vegetables and a good magazine to relax with.

Here in a lovely corner shaded by magnificent trees, you will be able to relax and enjoy the pretty patchwork with its elegant rose pattern in delicate pastel shades

To make yourself really comfortable in the open, make sure to bring a romantic patchwork quilt along. And if there is space, take a cushion in case you feel like a nap after the meal. You should also bring a sunhat and some light reading. Fill the picnic basket with all kinds of delicacies: fruit and crisp vegetables should definitely be included. and of course also salads, bread and spreads. Also bring cutlery, glasses, cups and napkins. Complete the picnic menu with refreshing drinks such as home-made herb tea. For later in the afternoon, bring coffee and home-made cakes.

For a romantic setting (if have enough room in the picnic basket), you can bring candles and tea lights to create a special atmosphere, and of course a little vase for freshly picked wild flowers!

85 top An old metal colander is used as cachepot. The old china and the tea towel with a red stripe complete the nostalgic effect of this decorative arrangement.

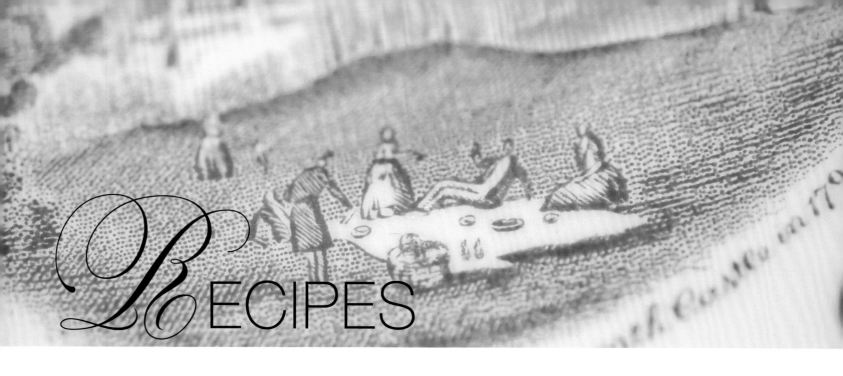

RECIPES

LAYER SALAD

Ingredients for 1 jar (1-2 people):

1 boiled egg, ½ cucumber, 2 small scallions, a small bunch of radishes, 3½ oz (100 g) cherry tomatoes, 1 small red pepper, 1 small nectarine, 1 oz (50 g) diced ham, 1 small bunch chives.

For the dressing:

2 tbsp sunflower oil, 1 tbsp mayonnaise, 1 tsp mustard, a little natural yogurt, salt, herbs and pepper.

Decoration:

Fresh edible flowers such as pansies and chopped chives.

Method:

Peel the egg and cut into small pieces. Peel the cucumber and scallions, then cut them and the radishes, cherry tomatoes, red pepper and nectarine into small pieces.

For the dressing, mix together the sunflower oil, mayonnaise, mustard and natural yogurt and season with salt, pepper and herbs. Arrange the eggs, the small vegetable and fruit pieces as well as the diced ham layer by layer until the jar is full. Spread a little dressing on each layer. Cover and leave to stand for a while so the flavors blend. Garnish with the edible flowers and chopped chives.

FORTUNE TEA

For 2 pints (1 liter)
Herb tea
a little elderberry syrup
1 nectarine
1 lemon
3-4 fresh mint leaves
a little sugar

Method: Prepare 2 pints (1 liter) of the herb tea of your choice. Add a little elderberry syrup and leave to cool. Cut the nectarine into small pieces, cut the lemon into quarters and add the fruit together the mint leaves. Put in the refrigerator and leave for a few hours. Then add sugar to taste.

BUNDT CAKE WITH CHOCOLATE CHIPS

Ingredients:
*1 cup+2 tbsp (250 g)
butter
2 cups (250 g) flour
1 sachet baking powder
1 cup+2 tbsp (230 g)
sugar
4 eggs
zest of 1 untreated lemon
1 bar of chocolate
(72% cocoa), chopped*

Method: Whisk the butter until foamy. Mix the flour and baking powder together. Separate the eggs. Stir the egg yolks and sugar together, then add the flour and stir to obtain a smooth dough. If the dough is too firm add a little milk or cream. Now add the grated lemon zest and chopped chocolate. Beat the egg white until stiff and fold into the dough.

Butter and flour the bundt mold generously. Add the mixture, then bake at 430°F (220°C) for about 45 minutes.

89 left Even when eating outdoors you can
embellish the table with old silver flatware
and fabric napkins. Every day is a feast!

89 right A home-made Linzer torte makes
a delicious sweet snack. And if you leave it in the
mold it was baked in, it is easy to transport.

CHECKLIST FOR A SUCCESSFUL PICNIC

Let yourself be inspired by my list. But don't forget you can always add to
a list. Just take along what your heart fancies

* a cozy picnic blanket
* crockery, flatware, glasses, coffee cups
* napkins and a small tablecloth
* a book or magazine
* a cushion
* candles and matches or a lighter
* a vase for the bunch of wild flowers you are going to pick
* depending on the season, a jumper or blanke
* sunhat and sunglasses
* some delicious food
* drinks

And naturally a good mood, a touch of romanticism and the right company!

Oggi apro le mie ali
E sento che domani
mo volerà
stretto nell' abbraccio
una donna che l'ama...

Little details with
an enormous effect:
a room suddenly
becomes very inviting
with just a few touches
of fresh pastel colors
here and there.

LIVING WITH DASHES OF COLOR

Little dashes of color ...

... are like dotting the i's. We can use them as supporting elements, to emphasize something without giving the impression that the house becoming too colorful. Particularly in smaller houses or apartments, too much color can be oppressive. And yet, what would our world be without color? And who would dream of refusing a magnificent bunch of flowers in glowing colors or a delicate pastry in soft pastel shades because they do not go with the color concept of the room? There are moments in life when colors are important for us and give us energy. Have you noticed what colors you go for when choosing your clothes in the morning? Depending on our mood and state of mind, we choose different colors. Memories are also aroused by colors.

92 Here a china plate is placed on an upturned wine glass is used as a stand. The table decoration owes its particular charm to the colorful motley of plates, some inherited, others bought in flea markets.

93 Who could refuse dashes of color such as these? These pastries with their colorful frosting are almost too beautiful to eat.

94 *Why conceal such colorful suede boots in a cupboard? If you would like to transform your favorite boots into a vase, all you need do is to insert a narrow vase inside the boot.*

For instance, when I think of the color pink, I remember the candy floss I used to love so much as a little girl. When I think of bright green I smell the fragrance of spring, the fresh green that sprouts from the soil, sometimes having to fight its way through the still snow-covered earth. And when I think of pale blue I hear the roar of the sea and feel the fresh sea breezes on my face. To arouse old memories again you should have some splashes of your favorite colors in your home. Bring a breath of spring into your house or bring back your childhood memories of candy floss. Or a stretch of beach and some sea breeze from past holidays. A home always bears the signature of the people who live in it.

A romantic work desk can be fitted even into a little room. An old kitchen table, pale green vintage garden chairs and a few desk accessories such as the hole punch and the home-made bulletin board create an inviting atmosphere.

In a small room a little piece
like this little cupboard can be
a useful and decorative addition.

Eating
is a necessity,
enjoyment is an art.

FRANÇOIS DE LA ROCHEFOUCAULD

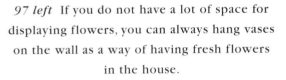

97 left If you do not have a lot of space for displaying flowers, you can always hang vases on the wall as a way of having fresh flowers in the house.

97 right Old treasures from the flea market such as this old glass soap dish and enamel wall bracket make excellent decorative objects.

The easiest way to add touches of color is to add home accessories such as cushions, lampshades or curtains. In the bathroom and kitchen you can use colorful hand towels or crockery in pretty pastel colors. Small pieces of furniture such as chairs or a single wall painted or wallpapered in a bright color have a similar effect. And fresh flowers in the right colors will add to the harmonious impression of the house.

98 top Ethereal, feminine, innocent … you don't need a special occasion to wear a romantic dress. Combined with accessories in pastel shades, the result is a feast for the eyes.

98 bottom These delicious macaroons in delicate pastel shades are almost too beautiful to eat.

99 top The bright yellow coffee cups with coffee jug are a classic from the 1950s that you might find in an antique market. At breakfast these will immediately put you in a good mood.

99 bottom Colorful paper napkins embellish the table and add to the decorative effect. The modern black and white stripes combined with the purist shape of the butter dish and the nostalgic design of the old sugar bowl result in a unique decoration.

100 A motley of decorative elements such as the coffee table book and the glass bowl with biscuits add a special touch to the atmosphere.

---

101 top The decorative romantic cones made from white card have been perforated so that the illlumination of the tea lights can be seen. Hanging from the wall, the soft candlelight creates a beautiful atmosphere.

---

101 bottom A room straight out of a fairy tale! Everything has been designed to look romantic, a little paradise in matching shades with many soft pastel touches. Above the table is a sumptuous faceted crystal chandelier. Moro the mongrel is comfortable on the sofa with its country-style gingham cover.

Left page: A comfortable Recamier chair with romantic accessories provides a cozy corner inviting you to read and relax.

The
very greatest
happiness in
life is the
knowledge
that one is loved.

ANONYMOUS

ELCOME TO THE
GARDEN ROOM

This bright gazebo invites
you to linger. It has been
furnished with a selection of
small pieces of furniture and
accessories such as cushions
and covers in various shades
of white and cream.

In the garden ...

... there is always something to discover. Anyone who is fortunate enough to have a small garden can enjoy nature all the year round. In spring, as nature awakens, the birds begin to chirp and the first snowdrops appear, you also become aware of the first warm rays of the sun. And you can observe nature from the comfort of the conservatory or the summerhouse. In summer when the days are getting longer and warmer, you will enjoy sitting in a shady place, perhaps under an apple tree or in the summerhouse. Everything smells of summer. The birds are enjoying the birdbath. How about a candlelit summer party with friends? With garden furniture, comfortable cushions and garden accessories the garden is swiftly transformed into a festive green haven. And if a summer storm should threaten the party, everyone can take refuge in the summerhouse. In autumn the colors in the garden become even more intense before the trees and shrubs eventually lose their leaves in winter.

Many birds have packed their bags for their long journey south to warmer climes. Meanwhile we can enjoy the last warm rays of the sun, if necessary wrapped in a soft blanket holding a warming drink. Then with the first

106 A pleasant little corner in which to soak up the sun and recharge the batteries. The scent of the lavender and roses invites you to relax in the deckchair and dream.

107 The patinated furniture, the white decorative objects, the romantic touches and a sea of flowers here create a divine shabby-look garden that you can enjoy on your own as well as with family and friends.

108 left A summer dream with a few red touches. The charming bench in white-painted metal with evident signs of age and use is a real shabby-chic piece.

108 right In summer the rose is the queen of the garden. These intensely scented red ones will create a passionate summer melody for the senses!

109 A secluded corner, perfect for sitting and seeing what is happening in the garden. This dainty little table is ideal for afternoon coffee or tea. The elegant old chair was bought in a flea market and painted white.

frosts everything becomes still in the garden. From the warmth of your house you can now watch nature slowly going to sleep. The pond may be covered with a thin sheet of ice and snow can transform the trees and shrubs into white beauties. Soon everything will be sparkling and glittering in the festive atmosphere. And with the addition of numerous candles and lanterns, the garden is ablaze with romantic lights.

THE DREAM OF THE SUMMERHOUSE

A summerhouse is a personal expression within your garden. A little paradise within a paradise. It doesn't matter how small it is—the main thing is that it has a roof so you can take refuge in it if it rains, and continue dreaming. Or you can enjoy a good book or magazine there, or relax with a cup of tea and a slice of cake. Comfort is very important and in winter you can achieve this with warm blankets and burning candles, while in summer some old sheets blowing the wind will provide a refreshing breeze. Depending on the season, you can vary the decoration and furnishings of the summerhouse. Create yourself a haven of peace in which you can enjoy your garden paradise all year round.

110 The garden is constantly changing and revealing new faces. In summer it gives us magnificent roses such as the fragrant varieties "Mary Rose," "Jacques Cartier" and "Heritage." Olive trees are also a must in the shabby-look garden because of their seductive Mediterranean connotations!

111 Time for a summer fairy tale! An old child's bed like this one makes a wonderful haven of peace for romantic day dreamers, whether to read a book or to have a short nap. The head and foot of the bed can be decorated to reflect the season, for instance with plants in little zinc buckets.

112 A delightful spot in the garden! A summerhouse is a romantic place and at the same time a magnificent eye-catcher in the garden! It can be used and decorated in different ways depending on the season.

113 top left White china crockery arranged decoratively on the old shelves, waiting for the next coffee break. Dainty glasses with floral motifs harmonize perfectly with the garden, hinting at the next garden party. Open shelves like these are useful for storing all kinds of useful objects.

113 top right Here is where the more delicate items used in the garden are stored, such as sun hats for sunny days.

113 bottom left A tempting display of cupcakes with blackberries from the garden. The romantic lacy tablecloth and dainty accessories add a touch of elegance and nostalgia that is an encouragement to dream.

113 bottom right The summer-house can be used whatever the weather. This vintage wooden armchair was rescued from a dumpster and given a new seat cover made from old sheets. The old window frame is used as a bulletin board for postcards and the like.

There, where my heart is my home.

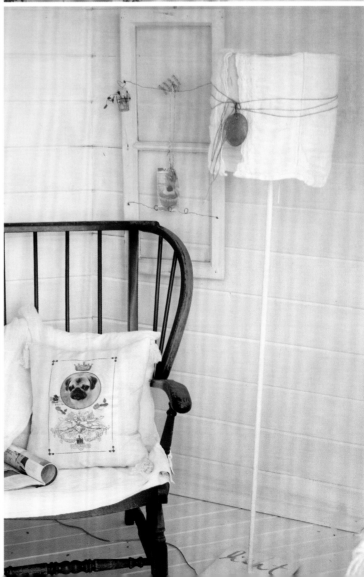

114 Old office drawers are perfect for a shabby-look decor as they make ideal containers for romantic arrangements in pale, soft colors such as spring-green and white. The small compartments are ideal for storing little glass bottles, vases, candles and much more.

---

115 top Surrounded by lush greenery in the middle of a floral paradise, no one could resist the romantic charm of these white chairs and the little table with its elegant tulle tablecloth. A perfect place to treat yourself to a refreshing, summer-colored drink.

---

115 bottom A sensuous garden haven! In late summer you will admire the grapes on this beautiful vine that also provides some pleasant shade.

The transparent curtains let the sun shine through but prevent wasps and other insects settling on the food on the table. And naturally the white tablecloth embellished with lace adds a special touch of elegance.

A country idyll: vine tomatoes, herbs and bell peppers straight from the garden. Everything is within reach in the summer kitchen.

THE SUMMER KITCHEN Life is much too short to have just a couple weeks' holiday. Enjoy the summer and all its facets, including in a culinary sense, and take a break from everyday life. But you can also enjoy a holiday at home in your own garden—every day! For me summer is closely associated with Italy. When I was a child, we spent most summers with our relatives in "La Bella Italia." I remember those wonderful summer evenings when the whole family would cook outside in the specially set-up summer kitchen. Set among olive, almond and lemon trees, this outdoor kitchen was quite basic without any modern kitchen aids, and yet the lady of the house, "Nonna," our grandmother, cooked the best food in the world. Of course she used natural ingredients such as fresh herbs, newly pressed olive oil and fragrant Parmesan cheese... There was an old stone oven in the summer kitchen where the bread was baked. Shortly after it came out of the oven, the still-warm bread was sliced and sprinkled with olive oil, then a few grains of coarse sea salt and finally some fresh rosemary, picked just a few minutes before—deliciously aromatic! Then the whole family gathered round the table and, like all Italian families, spent noisy, unforgettable evenings beneath the starry sky.

Open shelves and lovingly chosen decorations are traditional features in a real "country kitchen." A few kitchen utensils hang from the old enameled wall-shelf, found in a flea market.

Prepare some delicious bruschetta with a topping of fresh tomatoes, onions, basil leaves and olive oil. The wire egg basket is ideal for storing onions.

This Italian atmosphere can be recreated in your own garden by introducing a few atmospheric decorations and having a summer kitchen where you can cook in the open in the summer. It is wonderful when the fragrance of the fresh ingredients spread sthroughout the garden. To ensure you can fully enjoy the sensuous delights of cooking outdoors and you don't have to run constantly indoors, you must make sure that everything you need to prepare the meal is at hand. Besides all the usual basic kitchen equipment, you should have a range of fragrant herbs and fresh herbs which you can store in all kinds of jars. Whether home-made noodles, fresh bruschetta or a crisp salad, cooking outdoors is always an experience. Pay special attention to details when you decorate the table, arrange for some atmospheric background music, light some garden torches and invite family and friends to spend an unforgettable evening together!

Less is often more!
Freshly baked bread with sesame
seeds and a few herbs is not only
healthy but also very delicious.
Cachepots with patina add a touch
of nostalgia in the garden room.

An endearing shabby chic composition. The kitchen scale is very old, but it is still in use and cuts a great figure!

Home-made noodles
are a feast for the eyes
and the palate.

In our family recipes for various
delicacies are passed down from
generation to generation—as was the
case with my mother Lina and me.

HOME-MADE EGG NOODLES

Ingredients for 4 people:
3 cups (400 g) flour
4 eggs
salt
pasta machine

Method: Sift the flour, add the eggs and mix well. Add a little salt and knead the mixture with your hands until the dough becomes smooth and compact. Shape the dough into a ball, enclose it in plastic wrap and leave in the refrigerator for about 30 minutes. Then make the egg noodles with the pasta machine.

Maritime simplicity: stones polished by sea water combined with rings symbolizing love create a romantic still life. Opposite, a couple of my favorite pieces in pale blue.

$\mathscr{L}$IVE ★ LAUGH ★ LOVE

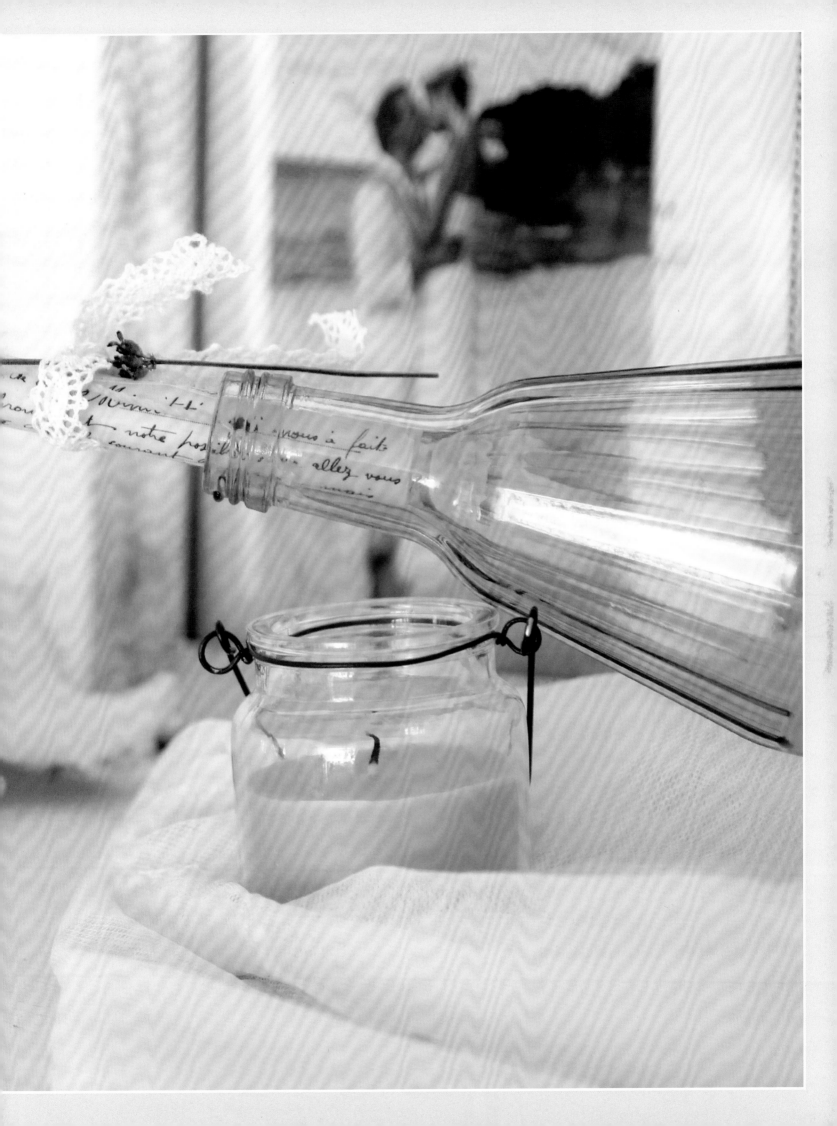

Live – La Dolce Vita style

What is more exciting than setting off on a picnic on a beautiful Sunday, having filled a small case with all kinds of delicacies and drinks? Often you don't need to go very far to find a beautiful spot. My husband and I really enjoy these rituals that enhance life. We often set off on such excursions to enjoy a touch of "La Dolce Vita" together. We believe it is important to be aware of all the good things life offers us every day and to live accordingly. At the weekend, when have the time, we enjoy cooking together and trying out new recipes. In summer we cook in our summer kitchen and treat ourselves to menus that are not only delicious but also pleasing to the eyes. A dash of passion is also allowed. Often after we have finished cooking we dress up and start the evening with an aperitif in the garden. And who says that a romantic

126 What a wonderful day! The crisp green olives, preserved with herbs in olive oil, are easy to transport in a screw-top jar and their fragrance will remind you of summer whatever the season.

127 An old suitcase with nostalgic vintage stickers is perfect for transporting your picnic and it can be used as a little table while you have an aperitif.

128 The sun is shining, perfect for an aperitif in the garden. Home-made grissini, made from flaky pastry, are wrapped with arugula and dry-cured ham—a gourmet delight! Top it off with flakes of Parmesan cheese to complete the experience. Served in old-fashioned preserving jars, these delicacies are also very decorative.

129 This glade is the perfect place for a romantic rendezvous, and the vintage suitcase is ideal as a table for all the delicious tidbits you brought along. Enjoy this "Dolce Vita" sitting on the pretty white patchwork bedspread with a refreshing drink.

aperitif must always be enjoyed within four walls? We frequently enjoy ours in the garden or we get on my husband's Vespa scooter and ride into nature. I love beautiful clothes and life is too short to leave them in the cupboard until the right occasion arises. Every day should be special in life. Clothes and furnishings are a mirror image of your personality and I love it when everything is in harmony. Are you now interested in an excursion as a couple? Don't forget, a party is made up of the little things in life. I wish you many romantic moments together, whether in the kitchen, in the garden or on an excursion in the "Dolce Vita" style.

A child's smile is the most precious gift! The room bathed in a soft light and the old-fashioned teddy bear are invitations to go and play with little Linda.

Laugh-
little Linda

A little girl will look even
more beautiful in white,
romantic surroundings than
she already is naturally. On one
of my recent trips, I found a
delightful little summer dress
in Singapore, a white one of
course. It was love at first
sight and I knew that one
day a little girl would look
like a shabby-chic princess
in it. I did not want to miss
the moment when an excited
young child would put this
dress on. The little one with
whom I was to enjoy this
moment was Linda, nearly
two years old and the
daughter of a very old friend
of mine. The white shabby-chic

A child's smile is the most precious gift! The room bathed in a soft light and the old-fashioned teddy bear are invitations to go and play with little Linda.

133 left The miniature carousel, a trinket for children, evokes carnival rides of the past. Combined with clothes or postcards, such trinkets adds a nostalgic note to the surroundings.

133 right It is fascinating to watch a child who is discovering the world or who likes to dress up. The simple white sunhat is embellished with a hair band decorated with romantic roses.

dress fitted her like a glove. She really looked like a little princess. She also loved the toys and accessories I had chosen for her. She was interested in everything, showing a delightful curiosity and always cheerful. Throughout the morning she smiled at the camera for me. Linda gave me the world with her smile and her beauty!

134 This decorative arrangement in several shades of white consists of a romantic child's dress, decorated with girly satin ribbons and playful accessories such as chains or hair clasps.

135 top Anticipation is the best pleasure. Wrapping up presents is such a thing. Then what can be more rewarding than giving a present and watching it being unwrapped?

135 bottom A beautiful satin ribbon will turn every wrapped present into an eye-catcher. The musical score decorating the wrapping adds a nostalgic-romantic touch. Who would not want to discover that this present with its enormous ribbon is for them?

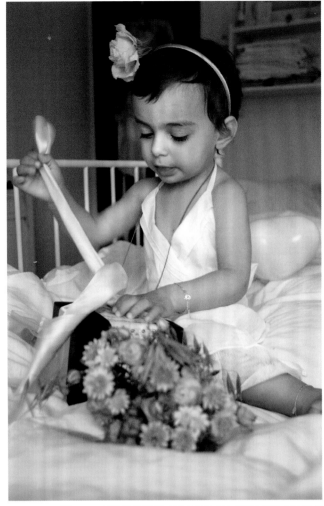

Declaration of Love

To love and be loved is the most beautiful gift on earth! What goes through your head when you think of love? Celebrating life, celebrating the day, celebrating love... With photographs you will immortalize the moment. Photographs reveal changes, feelings, moods and many details. They show the developments in our life and every day remind us of the people who are important in our life. Take some old or new photographs and arrange them on the chest of drawers in the living room and on the bedside table in the bedroom. And why not in the kitchen and bathroom too? Beautiful moments should be celebrated and shared. You will be amazed at how many memories you will evoke and how much conversation arises from them.

136 Photographs are memories of past experiences. The family gallery of black and white photographs looks very classy and nostalgic against the background of the off-white wall. All the picture frames have been painted white to enhance the harmonious impression.

137 Love letters are messages from the heart that are best written with a fountain pen. With its engraving, this classic writing implement is both an ornament and a companion for life.

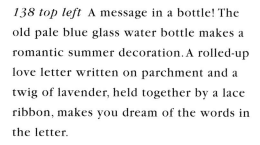

138 *top left* A message in a bottle! The old pale blue glass water bottle makes a romantic summer decoration. A rolled-up love letter written on parchment and a twig of lavender, held together by a lace ribbon, makes you dream of the words in the letter.

138 *top right* Symbol of love. The exchange of rings after the wedding vows will always be a unique and unforgettable moment.

138 *bottom* What would life be without laughter or love? An old piece of wood, three simple words and the key to life: live, laugh, love!

A ROMANTIC WEDDING Because of my romantic streak I love weddings. This is why there are plenty of photographs of our wedding arranged in romantic little corners throughout the house. Our wedding took place by the sea and when I close my eyes can still feel the breeze blowing in from the turquoise sea into the wedding pavilion. The water sparkled in the sun as did the gold wedding ring on my finger. And every day the magic of this wonderful day is conjured up by the pale blue notes that remind us of the sea and sky, the love letters, hearts and of course pearls.

Surround yourself with the colors of the sea! On top of a cupboard, which should not be too high, you can display some beautiful seasonal decorations. Display your experiences and decorate them with natural materials. In summer shells, pearls and candles in shades of pale blue will make a romantic maritime decoration!

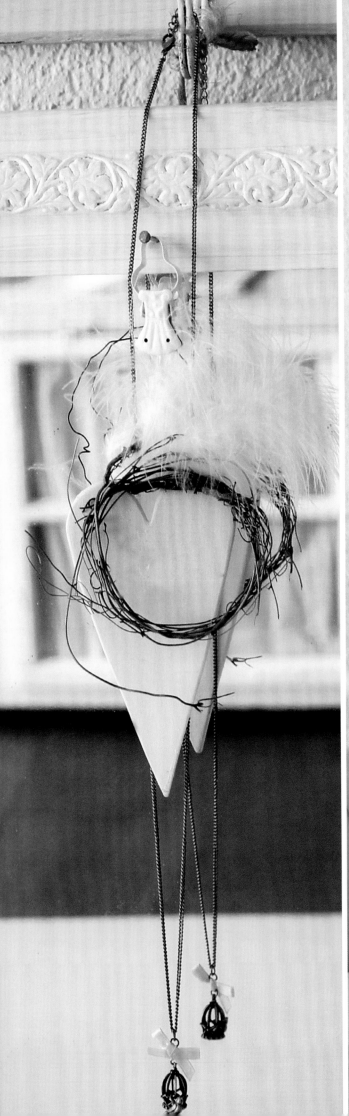

Love is a canvas furnished by nature and embroidered by imagination.

VOLTAIRE

My three treasures Paco Rabanne, Mai-Lin and Moro the mongrel. The three of them enjoy living with us on our "white cloud." By using bedspreads, removable covers and old sheets, bought at flea markets, a home furnished mainly in white is no problem, even with animals.

SEL AUX HERBES
20 KG. NET
1000

The feminine vanity
table with ornaments
and a shabby-look
mirror delights with its
delicate tones and playful
accessories. It is perfect
for every romantic
woman who loves to
pamper herself and to
live surrounded by little
details.

*F*EMININE
AND GIRLISH

The make-up chest

Even as a child I was fascinated by colors, fragrances and beauty creams. I could spend hours watching my mother putting on moisturizing cream, painting her nails red, applying make-up in front of the mirror and so transform herself. This make-up chest of drawers is like a tribute to the romantic woman. The many accessories, the various brushes and make-up tools, the dainty perfume bottles and fun jewelry lying on the dressing table reflect the personality of the woman using this piece of furniture. The objects on it include a little silver hand-mirror and nostalgic brushes and combs reminiscent of days gone by when women combed their long hair every night before going to bed and then threw a last glance at the mirror before going to sleep. Beauty is in the soul of those who look at it.

144 Floral poetry in pastel shades.
An old enamel bowl and china jug creates a mesmerizing atmosphere that conjures up " the good old times". A bunch of fresh flowers and spring twigs in pastel shades emphasize the feminine and romantic aspect.

145 A little box with fragrant pink powder for the lady of the house spreads its delicate scent throughout the room. As well as smelling good it transforms the bedroom into an oasis of beauty.

Fun jewelry such as these little rose-shaped stud earrings, combined with a pearl necklace, epitomizes the style of a romantic woman with a sense for detail.

"One must pay attention to the mind, because what is the point of a beautiful body if it is not inhabited by a beautiful soul," Euripides is quoted as saying. All the same, we still want to be beautiful, don't we? Choose your favorite perfume and moisturizing lotion and give them a place of honor on your dressing table. But above all, don't just look after your body, indulge your senses too! Then your inner well-being will radiate outwards!

This powder box with its fluffy powder puff was mine when I was a child. Today it is a decorative object on my vanity table and it reminds me of my childhood.

The fragrance of a woman's world... Home-made bath-salts with Himalaya salt and rose petals in elegant glass containers of various sizes adorn the bathroom.

148 A place where you can't help dreaming! A bunch of wonderfully fragrant roses in a bucket stands next to the open wardrobe with clothes in white and pastel shades. Perfectly in tune with the scene is a metal garden chair with a floral cushion while a romantic bridal veil embellished with white silk roses serves as a curtain for the window.

149 top Shabby-style costume jewelry is very pretty so it can be used to decorate the mirror where it is always within reach when you want to wear it.

149 bottom Glorious white brings light into a room and makes it look bigger. Here the soul will find serenity, and the white walls and furnishings set off decorative elements on the vanity table. Poetry for every day!

When imagination blossoms…
Looking at the graceful ballerina
one can almost hear the sound of the
piano in the background. The salmon-
colored ballet shoes and delicate tulle
complete the romantic atmosphere.

ROMANTIC IMPRESSIONS OF BALLET

Who among you has never dreamt of becoming a ballerina? Being a ballet dancer is the ambition of almost every romantic little girl, is it not? When I was young my bedroom was decorated with pictures of ballerinas. I still have one of those pictures, a picture of a dainty, graceful ballerina, dressed in an elegant, powder-colored tutu. Her dance pose is dreamy while her gaze is nostalgic and innocent. The picture reminds me of those wonderful time when I saw the world with innocent eyes. It reminds me of ballet classes and melodies on the piano. Ballet has a soothing effect, with elegant dancers moving like butterflies to the sound of the music. Feather-light movements that inspire, giving one the feeling of floating on a cloud. Passion finds expression in dance with its disciplined techniques and the precision of its movements. The semi-transparent dresses enveloping the bodies seem to be blown by a gentle breeze. Symbolic of it all are the ballet shoes with satin ribbons in elegant colors such as broken white, ivory or pink. That is why I love to display old treasures

152 A tutu, ballet shoes, a post card with a romantic view of Paris and elegant jewelry form a decorative ensemble on the piano.

153 *left* Candlelight can be used to create an atmospheric effect. For instance, you can wrap some thin wire round a thick candle, decorate it with a suitable trinket and place the arrangement in a soup plate with a gilded border.

153 *right* Sumptuous clothes with tulle, lace, pearls and roses add a romantic touch to the room and are a real feast for the eyes. The ballet shoes are incredibly romantic.

---

such as the ballet dress from my childhood. They are precious memories and it would be a pity to hide them away in the attic. In any case, decorative arrangements with ballerina tutus and ballet shoes, combined with ballet pictures or nostalgic jewelry create a magical effect and they have as soothing an effect as a ballet performance. Instead of pictures, you can decorate your walls with ballet dresses and ballet shoes. In this way you can create the most romantic still lives that will suit any room, whether a bedroom or living room, or to liven up a gloomy hallway. One of my favorite ballet decorations is on the piano, with its shiny black color making a giant splash in the living room. Embellished with a few decorative elements and with the lid raised, it is less dominant and at the same time it is a constant reminder of my childhood dream of becoming a prima ballerina.

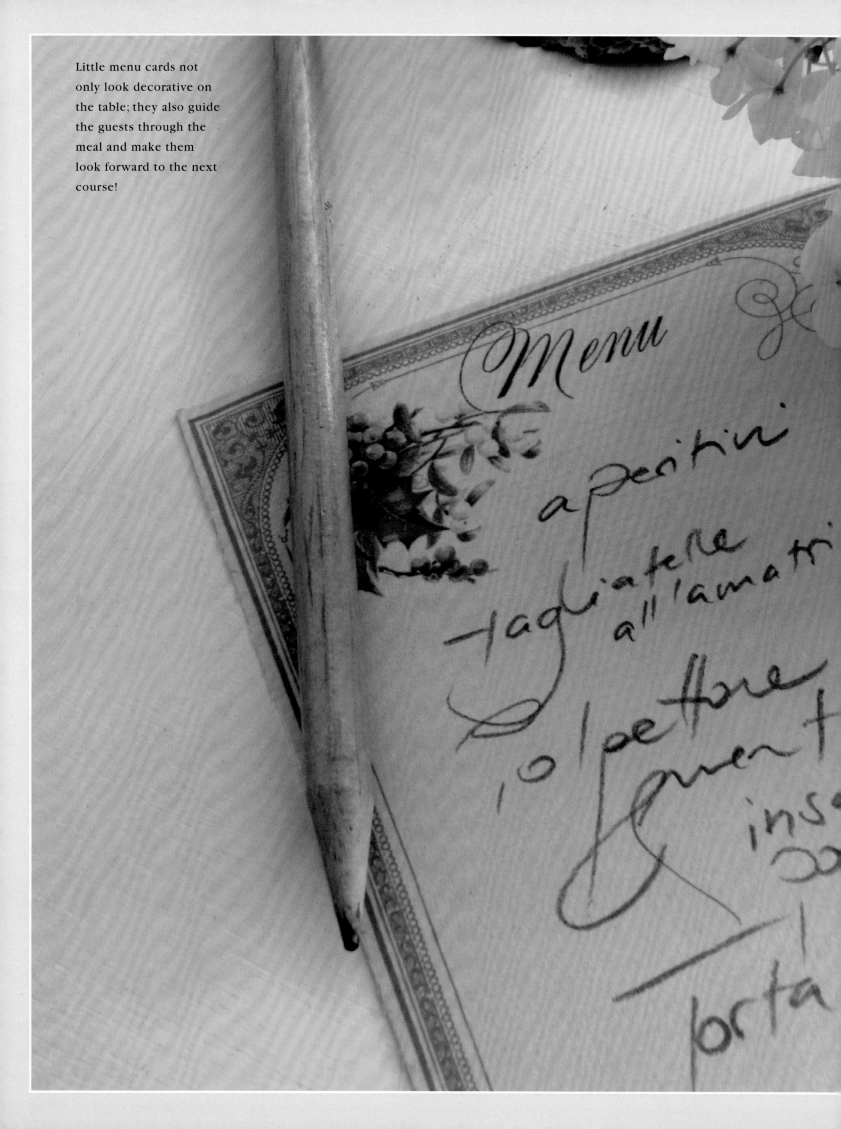

Little menu cards not only look decorative on the table; they also guide the guests through the meal and make them look forward to the next course!

RECIPES FOR THE SENSES

Meatloaf Nonna style

TOMATO SAUCE ALL'AMATRICIANA

for 4 people

7 oz (200 g) pancetta
1 onion, peeled
1/2 red chili pepper, finely sliced
1 cup + 3 tbsp (300 ml) strained tomato sauce
Herbs such as basil or parsley
1 pinch each salt and sugar
2 cloves of garlic

Cut the pancetta and onion into thin strips and fry in a pan together with the finely sliced chili pepper.
Add the tomato sauce and season with the herbs, salt and sugar.
Simmer the sauce on a low heat for about 20 minutes. Garnish with grated Parmesan and a few basil leaves.

Tomato sauce all'Amatriciana

PUFF PASTRY STICKS

for 4-6 people (photograph page 128)

1 packet oven-ready puff pastry (rolled up)
1 egg yolk
a few slices of dry-cured ham
a few arugula leaves and Parmesan shavings for the garnish

Roll out the puff pastry, cut into strips as thick as your thumb and brush with egg yolk. With your hands, shape the strips into elegant spiral shapes. Bake in the oven with top and bottom heat at 390°F (200°C) for 15 to 20 minutes, until the sticks are a beautiful golden brown. Remove and leave to cool. Place the arugula leaves on the slices of ham and wrap round the puff pastry sticks. Put some Parmesan shavings in the bottom of a large glass and put the puff pastry sticks in it.

MEAT LOAF NONNA STYLE

for 4 people

2 slices white bread
1 lb 2 oz (500 g) ground beef
3 eggs
13/4 oz (50 g) freshly grated Parmesan
some mint leaves
spices, salt
some sunflower oil for the mold

Soak the slices of bread in a little water. Season the ground beef, add the eggs, Parmesan and mint leaves and mix together well. Squeeze the bread to remove the liquid, cut into small pieces and add to the mixture. Knead all the ingredients and shape into a loaf. Grease the baking mold with a little sunflower oil. Preheat the oven to 450°F (230°C) and bake the meatloaf for about 30 minutes until golden brown.

HOME-MADE BASIL PESTO

makes about 1/2 cup (125 ml)

2 tbsp pine nuts
3 cloves garlic
1 bunch of basil
13/4 oz (50 g) freshly grated Parmesan
3 tbsp (50 ml) olive oil
some salt

Roast the pine nuts in a pan without fat until golden brown. Leave to cool. Meanwhile peel the garlic cloves, wash the basil and pat dry. Put the pine nuts in a large bowl together with the garlic, basil, Parmesan and olive oil. Puree with an immersion blender. Season with salt..

OLIVES WITH BASIL PESTO

for 2-4 people

1 small jar olives, 8 oz (220 g) drained
about 1 oz (25 g) shelled walnuts
3-4 tbsp pesto (see recipe above)
1-2 tbsp olive oil

Drain the olives thoroughly. Chop the walnuts and stir into the olives together with the pesto and olive oil. Then leave the olives to stand for about 1 hour (photograph page 126).

STUFFED PIADINE SLICES

for 2-4 people

2 pieces piadina (Italian flatbread)
31/2 oz (100 g) salami, thinly sliced
13/4 oz (50 g) Stracchino cheese

Cover one piadina with sliced salami and stracchino cheese. Put the second piadina on top, then cut the stuffed piadina into eight triangular slices. They can also be served warm. To do this, heat the piadine briefly in a pan before cutting.

MERINGUE APPLE TART WITH ROSE HIP SYRUP

For the short pastry:
1 cup + 3 tbsp (150 g) flour
6 tbsp (70 g) sugar
1/2 tsp baking powder
a pinch of salt
1 egg yolk
5 tbsp (70) butter

For the filling:
about 5 medium-sized apples
2 tsp quark
1 tbsp sugar
2 egg yolks, 1 egg
2 tbsp rose-hip syrup
a little lemon juice

For the meringue topping:
3/4 cup (75 g) icing sugar
3 egg whites

Mix together the flower, sugar, baking powder and salt. Add the egg yolk and butter and knead to obtain a smooth pastry dough. Wrap the dough in plastic wrap and leave in the refrigerator for about 30 minutes. Meanwhile make the filling. Wash the apples, cut and core them, then cut into cubes. Then mix together with the quark, sugar, rose hip syrup, egg yolk and a little lemon juice. Roll out the pastry thinly and line a 101/2 in (26 cm) round springform mold, making a border 11/4 in (3 cm). Then spread the apple mixture on the short pastry. Bake in the preheated oven at 350°F (180°C) for about 40 minutes. In the meantime make the meringue topping by whisking the egg whites with the icing sugar until stiff. After 40 minutes, remove from the oven, cover with the meringue topping, then return to the oven and bake at the same temperature for another 10 minutes until the meringue is slightly colored (photograph page 77).

Fill your days with life,
not your life with days

A LOVING THANK YOU ...

... to my husband Andreas who has always believed in me and who has always encouraged me ever since we met. He has helped me with this book wherever he could. Andreas is a positive-thinking man with who I really enjoy life. Thank you with all my heart for being there, my darling! I also thank my mother Lina who has created wonderfully beautiful arrangements for my LISA LIBELLE studio. Many of these creations have been reproduced in this book. And thank you, Mama, for all the talents you gave me in the cradle. Thank you too to my sister-in-law Viviane Braz who also helped me enormously with this project.

I would also like to thank Christian Verlag, who made touch with me and believed in me. It has been a wonderful collaboration. A special thank you to my editor Sabine Scheurer, it was great working with you. She was always willing to lend a sympathetic ear and I always felt I was in good hands.

Thank you to my friend, the journalist Melanie Breuer who I met during a lifestyle assignment. It was friendship at first sight. She too believed in me, opened my eyes and encouraged me with her praise. Also a special thank you to Kaiser & Ritter and the florist Meyer, responsible for the photographs in the chapters In the garden of dreams, Feminine and girlish and From a Love for Detail. A warm thank you to the models too: my mother Lina, little Linda, Paulina Gwóźdź and my husband Andreas.

And last but not least I thank myself! I would never have thought that life would honor me with a book. I dedicate this book to all the people who love me. While working on this book I experienced a lot and I discovered many new sides of myself. It has been great fun, I have cooked, baked, created arrangements, decorated, photographed, written... Often people asked me what kind of book it would be. Would it be a lifestyle book? An interior design book? A book on decoration? The answer was: a little of everything, but above all a book about the joy of living!

THANK YOU also to those who have bought this book! I wish you many harmonious hours, accompanied by much romance and joy of living!

Au revoir, your romantic LISA LIBELLE

Concept, photographs and text: Anna Lisa Colaianni Evangelisti – LISA LIBELLE
Product Management: Sabine Scheurer
Text editing: Anja Hallam, Sabine Scheurer
Layout and typesetting: Kirsten Harbers
Cover design: Kirsten Harbers

© 2012, Christian Verlag GmbH, Munich, 1st Edition 2012

WS White Star Publishers® is a registered trademark
property of De Agostini Libri S.p.A..

© 2014 De Agostini Libri S.p.A.
Via G. da Verrazano, 15
28100 Novara, Italy
www.whitestar.it - www.deagostini.it

Translation and Editing: Rosetta Translations SARL

ISBN 978-88-544-0891-3
1 2 3 4 5 6   18 17 16 15 14

Printed in China